THE PROPHECIES OF NOSTRADAMUS

By Ryan Nagelhout

Gareth Stevens
PUBLISHING

Please visit our website, www.garethstevens.com. For a free color catalog of all our high-quality books, call toll free 1-800-542-2595 or fax 1-877-542-2596.

Library of Congress Cataloging-in-Publication Data

Nagelhout, Ryan.
The prophecies of Nostradamus / by Ryan Nagelhout.
p. cm. — (History's mysteries)
Includes index.
ISBN 978-1-4824-2090-6 (pbk.)
ISBN 978-1-4824-2089-0 (6-pack)
ISBN 978-1-4824-2091-3 (library binding)
1. Nostradamus, — 1503-1566 — Juvenile literature. 2. Prophecies — Juvenile literature. I. Nagelhout, Ryan. II. Title.
BF1815.N8 N34 2015
133.3092—d23

First Edition

Published in 2015 by
Gareth Stevens Publishing
111 East 14th Street, Suite 349
New York, NY 10003

Copyright © 2015 Gareth Stevens Publishing

Designer: Katelyn E. Reynolds
Editor: Therese Shea

Photo credits: Cover, p. 1 Apic/Hulton Archive/Getty Images; cover, pp. 1–32 (background texture) Igor Zh./Shutterstock.com; pp. 5, 11, 17 DeAgostini/Getty Images; p. 7 Sumaru/Wikipedia.com; p. 8 Fingalo/Wikipedia.com; p. 9 Italian School/ The Bridgeman Art Library/Getty Images; p. 13 Zereshk/Wikipedia.com; pp. 15 , 19 (Hitler) Universal History Archive/UIG/Getty Images; p. 19 (Napoleon) Samuel H. Kress Collection/National Gallery of Art, Washington, DC/Wikipedia.com; p. 21 (building) Rob Atkins/The Image Bank/Getty Images; p. 21 (Kennedys) Rolls Press/Popperfoto/Getty Images; p. 23 (Louis Pasteur) Albert Gustaf Aristides Edelfelt/The Bridgeman Art Library/ Getty Images; p. 23 (mushroom cloud) Science Source/Photo Researchers/Getty Images; p. 25 NASA; p. 27 Robert J Fisch/Moment Open/Getty Images.

Printed in the United States of America

CPSIA compliance information: Batch #CW15GS: For further information contact Gareth Stevens, New York, New York at 1-800-542-2595.

CONTENTS

Telling the Future..................................4

Who Was Nostradamus?.......................6

Turning to the Occult...........................10

The Prophecies 12

The Old Lion Falls 14

Burning Books and Death.....................16

Napoleon and Hitler.............................18

The Kennedys 20

War and Its Machines 22

To the Moon 24

Predicting 9/11?..................................26

The Unknown Future 28

Glossary..30

For More Information 31

Index...32

Words in the glossary appear in **bold** type
the first time they are used in the text.

TELLING THE FUTURE

The story of humanity consists of both wonderful and terrible events. Our history is filled with occurrences that have shaped the world. But what if someone could tell you about major events before they happened? What would you do if you could know what's coming next, rather than only being able to look back at history?

In sixteenth-century France, a man named Nostradamus became famous for his **predictions** about the future. Starting with his **almanacs**, Nostradamus made thousands of predictions, called prophecies, about future events. Over time, as some prophecies seemed to come true, many people became believers. Nostradamus is still mentioned today when events occur that recall his predictions. But who was Nostradamus? Was he truly a soothsayer capable of seeing into the future?

REVEALED!

Some people believe most of what scholars think they know about Nostradamus is just a myth!

A SOOTH-WHAT?

A soothsayer is someone who predicts the future. Many people throughout history have claimed to have this ability. From ancient seers to modern **psychics**, countless people have declared they have these special powers. "He who is called a prophet now was once called a seer," Nostradamus wrote to his son Cesar. "Strictly speaking, my son, a prophet is one who sees things remote [far] from the natural knowledge of men."

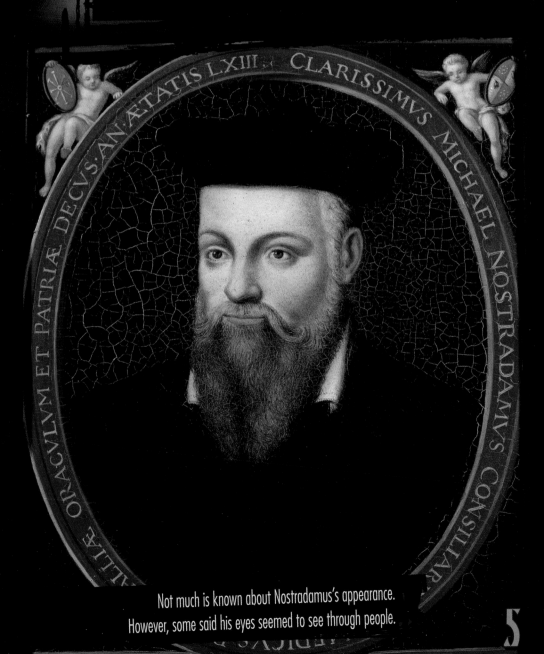

Not much is known about Nostradamus's appearance.
However, some said his eyes seemed to see through people.

WHO WAS NOSTRADAMUS?

The man known to the modern world as Nostradamus was born Michel de Nostredame (or Notredame) in Saint-Rémy, France, in 1503. Michel was a smart child who was educated by his grandfather, the same man who taught him about **astrology**.

When Michel was 14, he went to the university to become a doctor. Though an outbreak of plague forced him to leave the university, he received his medical license from the University of Montpellier in southern France in 1525. He then changed his last name to Nostradamus, the Latin form of his name. It was common for scholars to do this at that time.

Practicing medicine in Europe during the 1500s meant treating the plague. The "Black Death," as it was called, had killed millions and terrified the continent.

REVEALED!

The most common form of plague was bubonic plague, in which large swellings, called buboes, formed in certain parts of the body. It was spread when an infected rat or flea bit someone.

PLAGUE IN EUROPE

Nostradamus became well respected for a treatment for the plague that used rose petals and spices. He also made sure to be very clean, washing himself and his patients while treating them, which was probably why he had more success in his treatments than other doctors. However, while Nostradamus was traveling through southern France practicing medicine, his wife and two children died of the plague, which made people doubt his medical skills.

Many people think this building was the birthplace of Nostradamus.

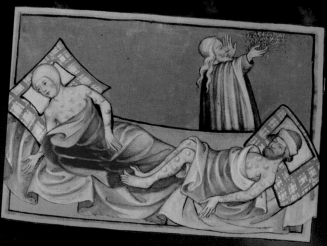
plague victims

Life and medicine in the sixteenth century were much different than they are today. Many doctors and other scholars believed in astrology. They thought the placement of the moon, sun, planets, and stars in the sky affected people and their health. These beliefs affected Nostradamus's later prophecies.

At that time, religion was a ruling force in France. Saying something offensive could result in getting called to an inquisition, a religious court that punished people for **heresy**. In 1538, Nostradamus was accused of insulting a religious statue and was called in front of an inquisition. But Nostradamus fled France to avoid the court. He didn't return until several years later, when he felt he was safe.

REVEALED!

Some believe Nostradamus didn't insult the statue—he insulted the sculptor!

One legend about Nostradamus's powers involves a prediction he made when traveling after the death of his family. One day while in Italy, he came across monks herding pigs. It's said that Nostradamus stopped in front of one monk, Felice Peretti, and kneeled down. He addressed him as "Your Holiness," a title for the pope of the Roman Catholic Church. In 1585, almost two decades after Nostradamus's death, Peretti became Pope Sixtus V.

The monk who would become Pope Sixtus V (shown here) was just a young man when Nostradamus was said to have predicted his future.

TURNING TO THE OCCULT

Nostradamus returned to France in 1547, settling in Salon-de-Provence. He married again and published two books on medicine. By 1550, he was becoming more interested in the **occult**. That year, he published an almanac containing predictions that became very popular.

Nostradamus began spending many hours in his study. He put water in a brass tripod, a bowl sitting on three legs. He stared into the tripod, just as the famous **oracles** of Delphi in ancient Greece were said to have done. Nostradamus claimed to see visions of the future and began writing them down. In 1555, Nostradamus published a book, *Les Prophéties* (or *The Prophecies*), the work that has especially fascinated people for hundreds of years.

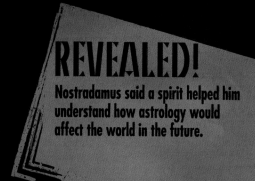

REVEALED!

Nostradamus said a spirit helped him understand how astrology would affect the world in the future.

ALL ABOUT ALMANACS

Almanacs have been written for centuries and were very popular in France during Nostradamus's time. The books predicted weather patterns and were used by farmers to grow crops. Nostradamus's almanacs made him popular in France and were the start of his predictions. But he's not the only well-known almanac writer. Inventor and Founding Father Ben Franklin wrote an almanac in colonial America during the 1700s. Called *Poor Richard's Almanack*, it had weather forecasts and puzzles and was published once a year from 1732 until 1758.

One of Nostradamus's medical books was a cookbook. It had recipes for plague treatments as well as makeup!

THE PROPHECIES

The Prophecies contained 942 four-line poems called quatrains. The poems were organized in groups of 100. Each group was called a *centurie*, or century. However, the seventh century ends at Quatrain 42. Nostradamus never explained why his work was lacking 58 quatrains.

The first two quatrains in *The Prophecies* describe the methods many seers used to look into the future. The rest of the work discusses a wide variety of topics and events. However, many quatrains were vague and confusing. Very few prophecies were actually explained in the text, but were left up to readers' many differing interpretations. It would take the death of a king a few years later for some readers to truly believe in Nostradamus's powers.

TRANSLATION TROUBLES

Nostradamus himself created many of the problems we have translating his quatrains into prophecies. He used different languages and even **anagrams** to mask his true meaning. Nostradamus wrote most of *The Prophecies* in French, but also used bits of Greek, Italian, and Latin throughout. He might have been worried his bold predictions about kings and powerful people could get him into trouble. His lack of clarity also helped increase the mystery that surrounded his work.

REVEALED!

One example of an anagram is the name "Chyren" for "Henryc," an older version of the French name "Henri." To make things more confusing, some of Nostradamus's anagrams seem to be missing letters!

The Prophecies became a very popular book in France, and many translations are still printed today. Nostradamus said his prophecies would forecast the next 2,000 years.

THE OLD LION
FALLS

The quatrain that first made Nostradamus famous is Quatrain 35 from Century I. In it, he predicts the death of an "old lion" in a one-on-one battle.

The young lion will overcome the old one
In a martial field by a duel one-on-one:
In a cage of gold his eyes will burst:
Two classes one, then to die, cruel death.

Nostradamus was thought to be warning Henri II, the king of France, to avoid battle. Four years after his book's publication, Henri II died in a **jousting** accident. His young opponent's lance went through the golden visor he wore, blinding him. After suffering terribly, Henri died 10 days later. Many felt Nostradamus's prediction had come true. Some wanted him killed, but Queen Catherine de Medici admired him and gave him protection.

REVEALED!

Supposedly, Nostradamus correctly predicted that three of Catherine's seven children would live to be kings.

ROYAL SUPPORT

Catherine de Medici read *The Prophecies* when it was published in 1555 and asked Nostradamus to explain some of the quatrains that she thought focused on her family. So, she was a believer even before her husband was killed. Nostradamus is said to have used a "magic mirror" to examine her seven children and make predictions about their lives. The queen consulted the seer many times about her future.

HENRI·R·II

LORGE

Seemingly predicting Henri II's death made many people in France believe Nostradamus could see into the future.

BURNING BOOKS AND DEATH

Predicting Henri II's death made Nostradamus and his prophecies popular in France. Nostradamus worked as a royal doctor and counselor for Catherine de Medici, but also continued writing prophecies in his study at home in Salon-de-Provence.

Nostradamus suddenly stopped writing quatrains in 1566. His health was failing by then. On the morning of July 1, he told his secretary, Jean de Chavigny, "You will not find me alive at sunrise." Nostradamus was found dead of heart failure on the floor next to his bed the following morning.

Though he lived just 62 years, his life's work gave countless people centuries of predictions to comb through. The body of the seer no longer lived, but his work was just starting to take on a life of its own.

REVEALED!

Nostradamus is said to have burned his ancient occult books before his death.

PLAGIARISM?

Many scholars have noted Nostradamus borrowed from other authors in *The Prophecies*. He used many of the writings of Plutarch, a Greek historian and biographer. Some of his quatrains used accounts and stories from the Bible. Several quatrains were taken entirely from other writers. Many writers at this time borrowed or copied from other sources without thinking it was stealing, though.

Nostradamus died in his beloved study, the room in which he made his many famous predictions.

NAPOLEON AND HITLER

Nostradamus made predictions about French and English kings of his time, but also about leaders born long after his death. His quatrains speak of very evil people he called *antechrist*, too.

In Quatrain 60 of Century I, Nostradamus wrote about an emperor born in Italy who would be known as more of a "butcher" than a "prince." Many people say this predicted the rise of Napoleon Bonaparte. Napoleon was born on Corsica, an island near Italy in the Mediterranean Sea in 1769. A soldier who later became emperor, he ruled France and much of Europe after many years of war.

Many people think that Nostradamus also predicted the rise of Adolf Hitler, the leader of Nazi Germany during World War II.

REVEALED!

Some quatrains predict opposite events. Either way, Nostradamus would be right about one of them!

HISTER OR HITLER?

Nostradamus wrote quatrains about war and a German man he called "Hister." Some say these quatrains seem to describe the infamous German leader Adolf Hitler. "Hister" is an old name for the Danube, a river flowing through Austria. Hitler was born in Austria in a town on the Danube. Hitler's leadership later sparked World War II (1939–1945), which would cause the deaths of millions of people and the destruction of much of Europe.

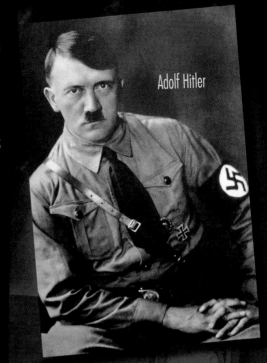

Adolf Hitler

Nostradamus is credited with predicting the rise and fall of Napoleon as France's emperor in the late eighteenth and early nineteenth centuries.

THE KENNEDYS

Believers in Nostradamus's work also think he predicted major events in US history. Although America, then the "New World," was only beginning to be explored shortly before Nostradamus's birth, some quatrains seem to speak of this place many years later.

Some people think Quatrain 37 in Century VI describes the **assassination** of US president John F. Kennedy, who was killed by a gunman shooting from a tall building in Dallas, Texas, in 1963. "From the roof evil ruin will fall on the great one," Quatrain 37 reads. It also said an innocent man would be accused of the crime. Some people think Lee Harvey Oswald, the man arrested for the murder, was innocent and that Kennedy's real killer was never found. Some researchers say Nostradamus predicted the assassination of Kennedy's brother Robert, too.

REVEALED!

Quatrain 37 in Century VI says, "A dead innocent will be accused of the deed." Lee Harvey Oswald was killed before he could be brought to trial.

Century I's Quatrain 26 is also said to speak of John and Robert Kennedy. It states a "great man will be struck down in the day by a thunderbolt." Later, "another falls at night time." President John Kennedy was killed during the day by a bullet in Dallas. Five years later, Robert Kennedy was shot at night in Los Angeles. Robert was running for president himself when a man named Sirhan Sirhan killed him.

Robert Kennedy (left) and John Kennedy (right) are thought to be the subjects of a few quatrains. However, there are other famous brothers who might be as well.

WAR
AND ITS MACHINES

Nostradamus didn't have the words to describe the modern machines of war, but many think he predicted their creation. Believers say Nostradamus foretold the development of rockets, submarines, and even weapons used in modern war. Quatrain 91 in Century II describes weapons being used to punish cities with "fire, hunger, and death," causing many to believe Nostradamus predicted the atomic bomb attacks on the Japanese cities of Hiroshima and Nagasaki at the end of World War II.

Some believe Nostradamus predicted the Gulf War between the United States and Iraq in 1991 in his Quatrain 86 in Century X. He may have called Iraqi president Saddam Hussein the "king of Babylon." However, the other "ruler" mentioned is the "king of Europe," which couldn't be used to describe US president George H. W. Bush.

REVEALED!

Some think Quatrain 86, Century X, describes a war yet to be fought in the Middle East: "Of reds and whites he will lead a great troop, And they will go against the king of Babylon."

Louis Pasteur

One quatrain Nostradamus scholars like to argue about is Quatrain 25 in Century I. Its first two lines are usually translated as: "The lost thing is discovered, hidden for many centuries. Pasteur will be celebrated almost as a God-like figure." Some believe "pasteur" refers to French scientist Louis Pasteur. The chemist proved that germs cause disease and also found a way to kill bacteria in foods, two discoveries that led to many people celebrating his accomplishments.

Quatrains about great explosions, fire, and underwater attacks are all credited with predicting war machines Nostradamus could never have known about.

TO THE MOON

Though Nostradamus and others studied astrology, sixteenth-century people knew little about space. There was no way for Nostradamus to know that men would one day walk on the moon, but many people believe his prophecies foretold that.

Nostradamus mentioned the moon in a number of quatrains, but believers point to Quatrain 65 in Century IX as the prediction of the US space program. Translations say someone will walk "on the corner of the moon." In 1969, *Apollo 11* landed on the moon and astronaut Neil Armstrong took humanity's first steps on alien soil.

Many claim the second part of the quatrain, which speaks of "unripe fruit," refers to the *Challenger* disaster of 1986. Seven astronauts died when the space shuttle exploded just 73 seconds after launch.

REVEALED!

Quatrain 81 in Century I is also thought to have predicted the *Challenger* explosion. However, it says that "nine will be sent away," which doesn't match the number of astronauts on board.

FAKING A COLUMBIA PREDICTION

On February 1, 2003, the NASA space shuttle *Columbia* exploded over Texas as it came back to Earth after a mission. Seven astronauts died in the accident. Soon after, a prophecy linked to Nostradamus circulated on the Internet describing an accident where "seven shall perish" over "the lone star." This "prophecy" was made up, though. It wasn't the first time an imaginary prophecy was connected to Nostradamus.

Did Nostradamus predict the success of *Apollo 11*? Some people think the quatrain really talks about setting up a moon base for people to live in!

PREDICTING 9/11?

When the **terrorist** attacks of September 11 destroyed the World Trade Center in New York City in 2001, believers in Nostradamus studied *The Prophecies*, searching for connections to the terrible event. Many looked to Quatrain 97 in Century VI, which described "fire" in a "great new city." The first verse says: "Forty-five degrees, the sky will burn." Some feel that the "new city" is New York City, which sits at 40 degrees north latitude, somewhat close to Nostradamus's number.

Quatrain 97 isn't exact enough to be proof that Nostradamus predicted the attacks on New York, but none of Nostradamus's writings were ever specific. Believing in his powers is a personal choice.

REVEALED!

Many towns in France are named *Villeneuve*, which means "new city." Could Nostradamus have been talking about an attack on one of these in Quatrain 97 in Century VI?

CHANGING THE FUTURE

Defenders of Nostradamus and his prophecies say that all his quatrains aren't supposed to come true. They say Nostradamus only predicted the worst that could possibly happen. Not all followers of Nostradamus believe the world will end in the plagues, earthquakes, floods, and wars he predicted would occur. They think we have the power to use his predictions as warnings and change the future for the better.

Do you think Nostradamus really predicted the terrorist attacks in New York City on 9/11?

THE UNKNOWN FUTURE

Those who believe Nostradamus was a true seer say over half of his predictions have come true in the more than 400 years since the publication of *The Prophecies*. They think the coming years will see more and more of his quatrains ring true. His writings refer to other evil rulers, and many think he even predicted the end of the world.

Many more remain **skeptical** of Nostradamus's prophecies. They say they're too unclear to point to a particular event. Others say bad translations over the years have confused the ideas in his writings. Some even say he wasn't making predictions, but simply commenting on events of his own time.

What do you think about the prophecies? Could Nostradamus see the future all those years ago?

REVEALED!

It's thought that one of Nostradamus's predictions foretold the deaths of some men who later broke into his tomb!

The mystery surrounding Nostradamus has made it easy to credit quatrains and false prophecies to the sixteenth-century writer. Every major world event seems to cause people to search for connections to Nostradamus. The Internet is full of false quotes from Nostradamus's writings and unreliable translations. Make sure you find trustworthy sources when searching through the prophecies of Nostradamus. Check out translated copies of *The Prophecies* from the library, or find an academic website when doing your own research.

A TIMELINE OF NOSTRADAMUS'S LIFE

1503 Michel de Nostredame (or Notredame) is born in Saint-Rémy, France.

1517 Michel begins to attend a university to learn medicine, but leaves because of a plague outbreak.

1525 Michel receives a medical license from the University of Montpellier and changes his last name to Nostradamus.

1538 Nostradamus is called in front of an inquisition and flees France.

1547 Nostradamus returns to France, settling in Salon-de-Provence.

1550 Nostradamus publishes an almanac containing his first predictions.

1555 Nostradamus publishes *Les Prophéties* (or *The Prophecies*).

1556 Nostradamus makes predictions for Queen Catherine de Medici and becomes a royal doctor.

1559 Henri II dies in a jousting accident, which is thought to fulfill one of Nostradamus's predictions.

1566 Nostradamus dies on July 1, after predicting his own death.

GLOSSARY

almanac: a book published each year containing facts about the movements of the sun and moon, changes in the tides, and other information

anagram: a puzzle in which a word or phrase contains all the letters of another word or phrase

assassination: the killing of someone, especially a public figure

astrology: the study of the positions of the moon, sun, and planets in the belief that their motions affect people

heresy: an opinion or belief that goes against official religious teachings

joust: a form of competition between two knights on horseback who try to unseat each other with a long weapon called a lance

occult: magic, witchcraft, or the supernatural

oracle: in ancient Greece or Rome, a person thought to have special power from the gods to give advice or tell the future

prediction: a guess about what will happen in the future

psychic: a person who is believed to have supernatural abilities or knowledge

skeptical: tending to question rather than believe

terrorist: one who uses violence and fear to challenge an authority

FOR MORE INFORMATION

BOOKS

Doeden, Matt. *Nostradamus*. Mankato, MN: Capstone Press, 2007.

Doft, Tony. *Nostradamus*. Minneapolis, MN: Bellwether Media, 2011.

Roberts, Russell. *The Life and Times of Nostradamus*. Hockessin, DE: Mitchell Lane Publishers, 2008.

WEBSITES

Nostradamus Biography
biography.com/people/nostradamus-9425407
Read more about Nostradamus and watch a Biography Channel documentary about him.

Top 10 Nostradamus Predictions
sciencechannel.com/strange-science/10-nostradamus-predictions.htm
Read more about the major world events people say Nostradamus predicted.

INDEX

almanacs 4, 10, 11, 29

anagram 12, 13

Apollo 11 24, 25

astrology 6, 8, 10, 24

atomic bomb 22

Bonaparte, Napoleon 18, 19

Catherine de Medici 14, 15, 16, 29

Challenger 24

Columbia 25

false quotes 29

France 4, 6, 7, 8, 10, 11, 13, 14, 15, 16, 18, 19, 26, 29

Gulf War 22

Henri II 14, 15, 16, 29

Hitler, Adolf 18, 19

imaginary prophecy 25

inquisition 8, 29

Kennedy, John F. 20, 21

Kennedy, Robert 20, 21

medicine 6, 7, 8, 10, 29

moon 24, 25

Nostredame, Michel de 6, 29

occult 10, 16

Oswald, Lee Harvey 20

Pasteur, Louis 23

plague 6, 7, 11, 27, 29

Prophecies, The 10, 12, 13, 15, 17, 26, 28, 29

terrorist attacks 26, 27

World War II 18, 19, 22